Cat and Dog wanted a snack.

Cat had a cup of raisins.
Dog had a cup of peanuts.

They poured in the raisins and peanuts, and they mixed it all up.

It was better than before,
but they wanted something more.

They called Mouse.

Mouse came over with a cup of pretzels.

He poured in the pretzels, and they mixed it all up.

It was better than before,
but they wanted something more.

They called Kitten.

Kitten came over with a cup of crackers.

She poured in the crackers, and they mixed it all up.

It was better than before, but they wanted something more.

They called Pup.

Pup came over with a cup of chocolate candies.

He poured in the chocolate candies, and they mixed it all up.

It was better than before, and they didn't need any more.

They each took a cup and divided it up.

It was better than before,
and they all got something more!